The Christmas Dream

A Christmas Story by Dennis Jernigan

Illustrations by Kim Merritt

innovo
PUBLISHING

Published by
Innovo Publishing LLC
www.innovopublishing.com
1-888-546-2111

innovo
PUBLISHING

Providing Full-Service Publishing Services for
Christian Authors, Artists, and Organizations: Hardbacks, Paperbacks,
eBooks, Audiobooks, Music, and Film

THE CHRISTMAS DREAM
A Christmas Story by Dennis Jernigan
Copyright © 2014 Innovo Publishing
All rights reserved.

Library of Congress Control Number: 2014956333
ISBN 13: 978-1-61314-266-0

Cover Design & Interior Layout by Innovo Publishing LLC
Illustrations by Kim Merritt

Printed in the United States of America
U.S. Printing History
Second Edition: May 2015

The Christmas Dream

A Christmas Story by Dennis Jernigan

A specially priced read-along version of this story narrated by Dennis Jernigan,
including an original Christmas song written and performed by Dennis Jernigan,
is available in the Audiobooks section of the eStore at innovopublishing.com.

Dedication

This book is dedicated to my children and grandchildren
and all the generations to come.

For days Judah had waited and watched for Christmas to get here. He believed that if it was snowing, it must be Christmas—and that on Christmas Day, it would automatically start snowing.

On this particular day, Judah was awakened early in the morning by his brother and sisters' announcement that snow was falling. Snow?! Judah could hardly believe it! It was the moment he had waited for! He ran to the window to see for himself that it really was snowing and then to his mom and dad's bedroom where, without even knocking, he burst through the door. "It's Christmas! It's Christmas! Mom, Dad! It's Christmas! It's snowing!"

Dad didn't want to disappoint Judah, so he didn't tell him that it wasn't really Christmas. But as soon as his older brother and sisters realized what Judah was saying, they firmly informed him that yes, it was snowing, but no, it was not Christmas and that Christmas was still twenty days away. This made Judah sad.

Since the children had already roused him, Dad decided to get up and take them sledding. Mom got the older children warmly bundled, and Dad got them and the sleds loaded into the van. Where they lived, there weren't many hills for sledding, so Dad would take them to the flood control field where the banks were about thirty feet high. With a good push, they were sure to have a great ride. All the way there, Judah talked about how everything outside looked like Christmas.

Several families were already sledding when they arrived. The children quickly unloaded and ran to the top of the hill. Hannah, Israel, and Annie had already slid down once by the time Judah and Glory made it to the top. Soon they were all speeding down the hill and running right back to the top as fast as they could. Several times Hannah went rolling off her sled as she crashed into the snow. Once Dad had the bright idea of piling all the kids on the sled with him! About halfway down the hill, they crashed into the snow and went rolling the rest of the way down.

As the morning wore on, Judah's laughter and fun turned to weariness and a cold nose! Dad knew it was time to go home when both Judah and Glory said they were no longer having fun. So Dad swept the snow off them with a broom, and they all loaded back into the van to warm up and to go in search of just the right Christmas tree. The mere mention of a Christmas tree brought warmth and brightness back into Judah's eyes, but only for a moment because Dad realized he had left his checkbook at home. This meant they would have to wait to get the tree another time, and it also meant that Judah was once again not having much fun. Things just weren't working out quite right.

Judah fell asleep as soon as they got home and unbundled. And I guess there's no need telling you what he dreamed of. That's right—Christmas! There were presents and parades and candy . . . But what made his dream really special is that he got to be with Mary and Joseph in Bethlehem on the night baby Jesus was born! Judah quietly knelt beside the manger. He wanted to see for himself just what made this baby so special that an army of angels would announce his birth. Mary smiled, and Joseph invited him to touch the baby. At first Judah was hesitant, but he placed his hand on the baby's face ever so gently. Then he caressed the baby's cheek with the soft touch of his fingers. (Judah had had a lot of practice with his new little sister, Raina Joy). And then he looked into the eyes of Jesus. Even though he knew it was impossible, Judah thought he heard baby Jesus speaking to him!

What happened next in Judah's dream was better than any Christmas he could ever have imagined. He was swept up into the clouds overlooking a magnificent city with streets of gold. Its buildings were made of fine jewels and precious metals. There was a river that looked like pure crystal. Trees along the river were loaded with luscious fruit. At the center of the city was a beautiful, bright light, and the voice he thought he'd heard coming from baby Jesus now seemed to be coming from that light.

As he drew nearer to the light, he saw a great white throne, and upon the throne sat a very kind and wise-looking older man. Though the man seemed loving and gentle, he had a look of sadness in his eyes. Without even thinking, Judah blurted out, "Why are you so sad?"

The man took Judah upon His lap and asked him, "Do you know who I am, Judah?" Judah shook his head no. "I am the Creator of the universe. I am the giver of dreams. I am your Heavenly Father. I am God. And you're right—I am sad. That little baby whose cheek you caressed is my Son. I'm sad because He was born to die."

"What? But why?!!" Judah was horrified. What he was hearing made no sense to him.

"A long time ago, I created the very first man and woman. I gave them everything they needed to be happy. (Remember, I made them, so I knew best what they needed.) I wanted them to love Me and trust Me and obey Me, but I decided to let them choose for themselves whether they would or wouldn't. Sadly, they listened to My enemy, who tricked them into loving him instead. As soon as the man and woman realized what they had done, they wanted to hide their guilt and shame. A little lamb was killed and its skin was used to cover them. Even now, My enemy still tricks men, women, boys, and girls into listening to him instead of Me, and every time they do, he makes them feel shame and guilt and pain. That's why I sent Jesus, my little Lamb, to be born on earth. His death would provide a covering for everyone who ever has been or will be tricked by My enemy."

Judah eyes filled with tears. "Jesus died? And you never got to hold Him again?"

"Oh, little Judah, yes, I did get to hold Him again. Because even though He died and was buried when He was a young man, he rose up out of the grave alive, and I got to hold Him again!"

"Then why do you still seem so sad?" Judah asked.

"Even though I sent Jesus to provide a covering for everyone who feels shame and pain and guilt over having been tricked by My enemy, many people still choose not to love Me—not to let Me hold them the way I hold my Son." He paused and then asked, "Judah?"

"Yes, God?"

"I want you to understand that you, personally, are the reason I sent Jesus to die. I made you especially for Me, and I want us to be together forever. You are the reason I built this beautiful city. You are the delight of My heart, Judah, and if you'll let Him, Jesus will keep you covered and protected so My enemy will never trick you and hurt you and cause you to love him more than Me."

And with those words, Judah found himself back in the stable, now holding baby Jesus close to his heart. (Only after what God had just told him, Judah felt more like Jesus was holding him.) How could this be possible? How could someone love him like that? To think that God loved him so much that He willingly gave His own Son to die in his place for his sins was, well, overwhelming! As Judah thought about what that meant for his life, he laid his head down next to the baby Jesus and closed his eyes.

The next thing he knew, Judah was startled from his thoughts by sounds of laughter and joy coming from somewhere outside the stable. Stretching and yawning and sitting straight up in bed, Judah realized he had been asleep.

Quickly he ran down the hall to the living room to tell Mom and Dad what he had seen in his dream, but his words were drowned out by the shouts of glee and laughter as Dad brought in the Christmas tree. For a moment Judah became so caught up in all the excitement that he forgot all about his dream.

After all the hustle and bustle of tree-trimming, eating, and filling the house with the sounds of carols and laughter, it was time for the family to head for bed. All the older children made their way to their rooms as Dad carried the younger ones to theirs.

When it was Judah's turn to be tucked in, his daddy picked him up and asked him if he had had a good day. That's when Judah remembered to tell him about his dream. He went through the whole thing, from the part about the stable and touching baby Jesus to being in the city of God. He didn't leave out a single part. And then he said, "Dad, I liked how it felt when Jesus held me in my dream. How can Jesus hold me in real life?"

Dad knew Judah was ready for the truth, so he spoke with great confidence. "Judah, you have to die to be held by Jesus. But the kind of death I'm speaking of is dying to yourself—giving up control of your own life and letting God be the boss—choosing to trust and obey and love only God, and never His enemy. Even when we try our best, we all mess up sometimes (God calls this sin), and our sin causes us to be separated from God. The Bible teaches us that death is the punishment for sin. But because God loves us so much, He sent His only Son, Jesus, to take the punishment of death for us. When Jesus died on the cross, He did so much more than provide a covering for our guilt and shame; He washed it all away!

If you believe in your heart that it was *you* whom God loved so much—that it was *your* sin that Jesus died for—that it is *you* who can be free from the punishment of death because Jesus took *your* place, then you can be held by Jesus! And no matter what, Jesus will hold you whenever you need Him to. Does any of this make sense to you, son?"

Judah sat there for a few moments as he thought how best to answer his dad's question. "Dad?"

"Yes, son?"

"I know I don't always obey you. I don't always do the things I know I'm supposed to. I know I'm tricked by the enemy sometimes. I . . . you know . . . disobey God. I've heard you call it sin. In my dream, God told me Jesus died for me. I want to love Him the way He loves me, but, Dad, I don't know how."

Judah's dad picked the boy up and sat him in his lap and said, "Son, Jesus did die for you—and for me—and for Mom and all your brothers and sisters. That's how amazing His love is. He says that if you confess with your mouth that Jesus is Lord and believe in your heart that God raised Him from the dead, you will be saved. That's how you love Him the way He loves you. In a sense, son, you die to who your were and rise again to be someone brand new—someone who loves Jesus."

Without hesitation, Judah said, "Dad, I want to do that right now."

Leaning into his dad's chest, he closed his eyes and said a simple prayer of faith to God: "God, I know I've listened to the lies of Your enemy. I know I've disobeyed You sometimes. But I know You gave Your son, Jesus, the best gift Christmas has ever known, to die in my place. I believe Jesus is my Lord. I believe You raised Him from the dead. And I believe You love me. And, Lord, I love YOU!"

Judah's dad stood with the boy in his arms and gently carried him to his bed. Outside, snow began to fall. Judah fell asleep and dreamed of Christmas all year 'round.

The End

www.ingramcontent.com/pod-product-compliance
Lightning Source LLC
Chambersburg PA
CBHW061355090426
42739CB00002B/34